To...

With love from................................

Date ....

Text copyright © 1996 Frances Grant
This edition copyright © 1996 Lion Publishing

The author asserts the moral right to be identified as the author of this work

Published by
Lion Publishing plc
Sandy Lane West, Oxford, England
ISBN 0 7459 3380 7
Albatross Books Pty Ltd
PO Box 320, Sutherland, NSW 2232, Australia
ISBN 0 7324 1352 4

First edition 1996

10 9 8 7 6 5 4 3 2 1 0

All rights reserved

Information about family records in Britain may be obtained from the Office of Populations, Censuses and Surveys, St Catherine's House, 10 Kingsway, London WC2B 6JP; the General Register Office for Scotland, New Register House, Edinburgh EH1 3YT

A catalogue record for this book is available from the British Library

Printed and bound in Malaysia

A LION BOOK

OUR FAMILY STORY

A Keepsake Album

Frances Grant

Introduction

'A family is a place with a Mummy and a Daddy,' said Zanna confidently.

'If you're lucky,' added Tom who, at eleven, thought himself vastly wiser than his little sister. 'I think a family is a group of people who are happy together.'

Whether we see the family as a fixed entity with x number of relatives, or a fluid network that is constantly changing, one thing is for certain: we all begin in families! What's more, we continue to be attracted to them, however far we may roam — invisibly drawn like bees to their hives.

This album begins and ends with family life in the present day, acknowledging the cheerful fact that for many people the family is still what makes life ultimately worth living. It's true that more of us are now single parents and half-siblings, yet our relationships with each other are just as important, and the love and the challenges that unite us are as keenly felt as ever.

As well as looking at the family today, however, it can be truly heart-warming to reflect on some of the distinctive, wise, eccentric and amusing aspects of our family cultures in previous generations. After all, what we are today commonly reflects the values and hopes of those who lived before us.

Fortunately, the enduring elements of family life are often good ones. There's the 'family wisdom' born of age and experience. There are common passions — travel, for example, or music, or a certain sport, or a particular set of ethical principles. There are special ways of celebrating certain family occasions. And there are shared patterns of spontaneity, friendship, hospitality.

These good traits endure partly because memory tends to filter out bad experience, but there is also a genuine drive in human beings towards what is fine and honourable. We really aren't attracted by the second-rate in life.

Sad times are, nevertheless, woven into the pattern. No family on earth has yet avoided the pain of tragedy, the desperation of conflict and struggle. Yet it is precisely through suffering that we grow in compassion and strength, and our minds eventually yearn again for what is positive and creative. Through companionship and in each generation we come to know resilience and courage. Our families are a rich heritage indeed.

Frances Grant

Here and Now

Crash, bang! The front door flies open and in falls our young hero. He's our tall, gangly footballer, star of the next generation, and currently trailing schoolbooks, headphones, and half a pair of spectacles. 'I'm starving!' he calls out happily, and he really believes it. Last month, it seems, he was a cuddly one-year-old; soon he'll be running his own life. But today, he's our young hero.

There are so many aspects of the here and now – the mundane as well as the sublime – that are precious. Catching sight of them is not always easy, especially when we are tired or preoccupied. But if we decide to stop and look for a moment, we will see a lot to celebrate: the energy, the quirkiness, and the sheer delight of different people developing in completely distinctive ways.

> *There is scarcely any less bother in the running of a family than in that of an entire state.*
>
> MONTAIGNE

Our Family Now

NAMES ....

....

....

....

DATE ....

MAJOR FAMILY EVENTS THIS YEAR ....

....

....

....

Here am I, and the children the Lord has given me. We are signs and symbols... from the Lord Almighty.

ISAIAH 8:18

Wherever you are, you should always be contented, but especially at home, because there you must spend the most of your time.

JANE AUSTEN

Dear friends, let us love one another, for love comes from God. Everyone who loves has been born of God and knows God.

I JOHN 4:7

Parents

Once we become parents, we enter parenthood for the rest of our lives. It is the most fixed of all human states, more than childhood, or marriage, or even belonging to a particular nation state.

For much of the time, parents work so hard at just being parents that they don't see their own strengths. Sometimes, however, it is good to put the humdrum worries of daily life on one side, and consider instead the wonderful contribution parents make to the next generation just by being themselves. God's purpose, too, is that of a loving parent. Surely there can be no more sacred purpose in life?

Mother and Father

MOTHER'S FULL NAME . . . .

FATHER'S FULL NAME . . . .

DATE OF MARRIAGE . . . .

OCCUPATIONS . . . .

. . . .

. . . .

SPECIAL GIFTS AND QUALITIES . . . .

. . . .

. . . .

. . . .

. . . .

The family that prays together stays together.

AL SCAPONE

*So we grew together,
like to a double cherry, seeming
    parted,
but yet an union in partition;
two lovely berries on one stem;
so, with two seeming bodies,
but one heart.*

WILLIAM SHAKESPEARE

Children

Talking once to my eight-year-old nephew, Hugh, I was struck by the extraordinary combination of wisdom and innocence that seems to mark out children from everyone else in society. We were talking excitedly about Christmas, and Hugh's eyes were growing wider and wider with eager anticipation.

Suddenly he stopped, and looked at me. 'Of course, I don't really believe in Santa Claus, you know. Because really, you see... I think he's the tooth fairy!'

Children have delighted people through the centuries — parents, teachers, family friends and relatives. The only strange thing, perhaps, is that we are surprised by this delight. After all, it is as children, and only as children, that we may ultimately experience the kingdom of heaven.

CHILDREN IN OUR FAMILY NOW

NAMES.................... DATES OF BIRTH............. DAYS OF DEDICATION/CHRISTENING..

....

....

....

....

....

....

I am fond of children (except boys).

S.D. COLLINGWOOD

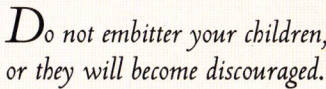

Do not embitter your children, or they will become discouraged.

COLOSSIANS 3:21

photo

SPECIAL CHARACTER TRAITS . . . .

. . . .

. . . .

. . . .

. . . .

. . . .

THINGS THEY HAVE SAID . . . .

. . . .

. . . .

. . . .

. . . .

. . . .

Our Roots

Superficially, family trees can seem rather dull – especially other people's! Tracing them in depth, however, almost always produces some treasure or other. See what can be found in your own, if necessary using some of the organizations listed at the front of this book.

Great Grandmother _____

Great Grandfather _____

Date of marriage _____

Occupations _____   *Grandmother* _____

Special interests _____   *Grandfather* _____   *Mother* _____

Date of marriage _____   *Occupation* _____

Great Grandmother _____

Occupations _____   *Special interests* _____

Great Grandfather _____

Special interests _____

Date of marriage _____

Occupations _____

Special interests _____

Children's children are a crown to the aged, and parents are the pride of their children.

PROVERBS 17:6

Great Grandmother _____

Great Grandfather _____

Date of marriage _____

Occupations _____   Grandmother _____

Special interests _____   Grandfather _____   Father _____

Great Grandmother _____   Date of marriage _____   Occupation _____

Great Grandfather _____   Occupations _____   Special interests _____

Date of marriage _____   Special interests _____

Occupations _____

Special interests _____

The child is father to the man.

WILLIAM WORDSWORTH

He that will have his son have respect for him and his orders, must himself have a great reverence for his son.

JOHN LOCKE

'*Do you know who made you?*' '*Nobody, as I knows on,*' said the child, with a short laugh... '*I 'spect I grow'd.*'

ROBERT LOUIS STEVENSON

Mother's Family...
Father's Family

'Remember your parasol, dear... and be quick, or the tram will have come and gone!'

Yes, society has definitely changed in the last sixty years, even the last thirty. Education, medicine, housing, language, politics, even money – all had different forms and values a few generations ago. Looking back over time, what was life like for those in previous generations of your family?

Father's Family

NAMES . . . .

Mother's family

NAMES ....

....

....

*N*ow the overseer must be above
reproach... He must manage his
own family well.

<u>1 TIMOTHY 3:2</u>

WHAT LIFE WAS LIKE FOR THEM. . . . .

....

....

....

....

....

....

> *History is the essence of innumerable biographies.*
>
> THOMAS CARLYLE

In Times Gone By

From the War to the winklepicker, from the ascent of Mount Everest to the first steps of man on the moon, the wider culture this century has shaped all our lives. Old family photographs were often taken on special occasions, linking people to the times in which they lived and giving us a glimpse of the connections that helped shape their lives.

Old family photos linked to major events

News clippings

> *P*rinting, gunpowder and the magnet... these three have changed the whole face and state of things throughout the world.
>
> FRANCIS BACON

> *H*eaven and earth will pass away, but my words will never pass away.
>
> FROM THE GOSPEL OF MATTHEW
> 24:31

EVENTS WHICH AFFECTED OUR FAMILY'S LIVES ....

....

....

....

DATES ....

HOW IT AFFECTED THEM ....

....

....

....

....

Unhappiness comes from this source... I mean the attempt to prolong family connection unduly and to make people hang together artificially who would never naturally do so. And the old people do not really like it much better than the young.

— SAMUEL BUTLER

My Giddy Aunt!

Did your grandmother climb the Andes? Did your cousin collect aeroplanes as a hobby? There are some legendary people in families! Some were wonderful storytellers, others made extraordinary choices in their work, and others again travelled to exotic countries and did what other people said were crazy things. But they had a special influence on our lives, however indirect, and we remember them with affection and, if we admit it, some admiration!

LEGENDARY CHARACTERS IN OUR FAMILY

NAMES..........................   DETAILS OF THEIR LIVES..

> *There are secrets in all families.*
>
> — GEORGE FARQUHAR

> *Your light must shine before people, so that they will see the good things that you do and praise your father in heaven.*
>
> — FROM THE GOSPEL OF MATTHEW 5:16

photo

A family likeness

*I like to be as my fathers were,
In the days ere I was born.*

WILFRID BLUNT

Have you ever been struck by the extraordinary likeness of two people in a family who've been born generations apart? Perhaps they have the same glorious red hair or rich dark eyes, perhaps just a striking resemblance to each other in general; or perhaps they looked almost identical as babies.

Families can also produce other similarities: one young person may turn out to have 'a marvellous voice, just like his grandfather', while another may have an insatiable thirst for travel like her aunt who set off round the world when she was just eighteen! Similarities can be both attractive or unattractive, of course, but at their best they can create a very special sense of belonging, and often give us extra confidence in what we offer to those around us.

PEOPLE IN OUR FAMILY WHO ARE UNUSUALLY LIKE ONE OF THEIR RELATIONS:

....

....

....

THE WAYS THEY HAVE BEEN SIMILAR . . . .

. . . .

. . . .

. . . .

. . . .

. . . .

The past and present here unite
Beneath time's flowing tides,
Like footprints hidden by a brook
But seen on either side.

ANON

To live in hearts we leave
behind is not to die.

J. CAMPBELL

A photograph then

A photograph now

What's in a Name?

One child was christened recently with over a hundred names! At the other extreme, not long ago in certain areas of northern Scotland almost every male in a village or town would have the same name. To avoid confusion at school, teachers would add the house-number to the ends of names, making James Buchan Forty-two clearly different from James Buchan Sixteen (the teacher probably being James Buchan Twelve!).

Whatever the name, there is also a meaning. My surname, Grant, means Stand Fast. So far so good. My maiden name, Gifford, means Fat Cheeks! Dictionaries of names are often fun, and always revealing.

Fortunately, God knows each of us by name in a deeper way; what he knows is the name of our heart and soul, and every facet of our unique character.

*The loveliest fairy in the world...
is Mrs Doasyouwouldbedoneby.*

THE WATER BABIES

SURNAMES IN OUR FAMILY AND WHAT THEY MEAN ....

....

....

....

....

....

FIRST NAMES IN OUR FAMILY AND WHAT THEY MEAN ....

....

....

....

....

....

*For when the One Great Scorer comes
To write against your name,
He marks — not that you won or lost —
But how you played the game.*

GRANTLAND RICE

Now a slave has no permanent place in the family, but a son belongs to it for ever.

FROM THE GOSPEL OF JOHN 8:35

A Place to Be

*I will arise and go now, for
always night and day
I hear lake water lapping with
low sounds by the shore;
While I stand on the roadway, or
on the pavements gray,
I hear it in the deep heart's core.*

W.B. YEATS,
THE LAKE ISLE OF INNISFREE

Most of today's motorways are on yesterday's farmland. It's hard to believe that cows were milked, that grain was stored, that apple-sheds were filled with rosy pippins, just here, just there, beneath the rugged concrete stretches that take our thundering juggernauts.

It's hard, too, to believe how long people took to travel from place to place — by steam train, brougham, penny-farthing, horseback. The poet Samuel Taylor Coleridge often walked the thirteen miles to see his friend William Wordsworth for breakfast; who would do that today?

We are fortunate indeed that we have no need to travel to meet our God. He is with us at all times, regardless of what place we happen to be at the time.

Photo of family travel in days gone by

PEOPLE IN PHOTOGRAPH . . . .

DATES . . . .

OTHER WAYS THEY TRAVELLED . . . .

PLACE..
....
DATE...

PLACE..
....
DATE...

Some of the places our family has lived

To travel hopefully is better than to arrive, and the true success is to labour.

ROBERT LOUIS STEVENSON

Be strong and stand firm. Be fearless then, and confident; for go where you will, the Lord your God is with you.

FROM THE BOOK OF JOSHUA 1:9

Traits that Endure

'Waste not want not.' 'There's no such word as can't!' 'Mothers are never silly.' (I like that one.) 'Thanks cost nothing.'

Do you smile because such remarks seem banal? Believe it or not, such instruction frequently has its roots in the great religious works of the world. The book of Proverbs in the Bible has many wonderful statements about good family traits (as well as bad ones!), and it's just one of many sources extolling hospitality, loyalty, friendship, moderation, and courage.

In many families, such sayings can have a subtle influence on entire behaviour patterns and these in turn pass down from one generation to the next. Have a think, and ask around. What are your own family maxims?

Delightful task! to rear the tender thought,
To teach the young idea how to shoot.

JAMES THOMSON

FAMILY ATTITUDES ABOUT STRANGERS ....

....

....

FAMILY ATTITUDES ABOUT HOSPITALITY ....

....

....

FAMILY ATTITUDES ABOUT LOYALTY ....

....

....

FAMILY ATTITUDES ABOUT WHAT TO DO IN TIMES OF HARDSHIP ....

....

....

FAMILY ATTITUDES ABOUT WORSHIP ....

....

....

FAMILY ATTITUDES ABOUT COURTESY AND KINDNESS ....

....

....

OTHER FAMILY MAXIMS ....

....

....

A mild answer turns away wrath.

PROVERBS 15:1

A merry heart makes a cheerful countenance.

PROVERBS 15:13

*B*etter a dish of herbs when love is there, than a fattened ox and hatred to go with it.

PROVERBS 15:17

Family Traditions

The old man sat in his hospital bed looking blissfully happy, and savouring the large piece of chocolate cake before him. It was his birthday. Someone had remembered. They always had chocolate cake on birthdays.

Family traditions can be so distinctive – the way Easter eggs are painted; the way names are written for important occasions; the time everyone eats together or the kinds of games that are played; the way that parties are planned or the particular music people dance to.

One enthusiasm so often fires another, and in this way families and indeed whole cultures acquire their own special characteristics. Occasionally, such traditions form a stumbling block, a snare because no one dares break from them. But more often, they provide special ways for celebrating just being a family.

If children do not find pleasure and entertainment at home they will seek it elsewhere, often in undesirable directions. Hence every parent should strive to make children feel that home is the happiest place in the world.

Games, pastimes and hobbies of all kinds should be encouraged; the young collector, naturalist, carpenter or engineer should find that father and mother are just as keen... The time and trouble spent in this way will be repaid a thousandfold in after years.

MRS BEETON'S HOUSEHOLD MANAGEMENT

THE GAMES WE PLAY ....

....

....

OUR SPECIAL FAMILY OCCASIONS, AND WHAT WE DO ....

....

....

FAMILY TRADITIONS ASSOCIATED WITH CHRISTMAS ....

....

....

FAMILY TRADITIONS ASSOCIATED WITH EASTER ....

....

....

> *Believe me, my young friend, there is nothing — absolutely nothing — half so much worth doing as simply messing about in boats.*
>
> THE WIND IN THE WILLOWS

> *There is a season for everything...*
> *a time for laughter...*
> *a time for dancing...*
> *a time for keeping...*
> *a time for loving...*
> *a time for peace...*
>
> FROM THE BOOK OF
> ECCLESIASTES, CHAPTER 3

So you have sorrow now, but I will see you again, and your hearts will rejoice, and no one will take your joy from you.

FROM THE GOSPEL OF JOHN

The sorrows of the years

All families know tragedy and struggle. Even the most fortunate families will at some time experience trials brought about by illness, harsh circumstances, and the hardships that touch us all.

The bright hope, however, is that even the bitterest challenge and suffering can produce the kind of growth and new life *which cannot otherwise happen.* As a real inheritance, we can treasure such gifts, and pass them on to those who follow.

Photographs

MEMBERS OF OUR FAMILY WHO ARE MUCH MISSED ....
....
....

TIMES OF PARTICULAR STRUGGLE IN OUR FAMILY ....
....
....

TIMES WHEN WE FELT WE HAD COME THROUGH ....
....
....

More marriages might survive if the partners realized that sometimes the better comes after the worse.

DOUG LARSON

God setteth the solitary in families.

PSALM 68

The Best of Memories

I once met a woman who had been sailing just offshore when her boat ran into trouble. Conditions were fine, and she was a strong swimmer, but she wasn't so sure about her ageing dog. It was a good mile or so back to the beach, and it was a slow business, with lots of reassurance and encouragement to her dog, to reach the sandy stretch just beyond the harbour. Afterwards, she was quite overwhelmed by relief and gratitude that both were safe and well.

Fortunately, there is a healthy human tendency to remember good times — adventures, holidays, sunny picnics, candle-lit services, a much-loved friend telling a good story over a special meal. Nor does it mean we wander round with unrealistic expectations about the future; just that we appreciate the good things that life has given us.

Photo of a memorable occasion

HOLIDAYS WE'VE HAD. . . . .

. . . .

. . . .

. . . .

. . . .

. . . .

. . . .

. . . .

The living God, who made heaven and earth and sea and everything in them, has shown kindness by giving you rain from heaven and crops in their seasons; he provides you with plenty of food and fills your hearts with joy.

ACTS 14:15

OTHER GOOD EVENTS IN OUR LIVES . . . .

. . . .

. . . .

. . . .

. . . .

. . . .

. . . .

. . . .

Come to me in the silence of the night;
Come in the speaking silence of a dream;
Come with soft rounded cheeks and eyes as bright
As sunlight on a stream;
Come back in tears,
O memory, hope, love of finished years.

CHRISTINA ROSSETTI

What a Disaster!

Accidents do happen. The inkblot on the final picture, the kitten on the roof, the chewed-up book and the car-keys in the lake are just a few incidents in my life which caused minor (and major!) upsets at the time. These things can happen to anyone, and when they do we rush around madly, trying to sort things out.

Later, sometimes a good bit later, we can laugh. We realize how lucky we really are to be able to lead such rich lives, and our misfortunes become a bridge of sober understanding – of those who suffer far greater disaster in the world.

Just as importantly, mishaps are also times for forgiveness, both of others and ourselves. And forgiveness is a balm we all need, every day of our lives.

EVENT..

....

....

....

....

PLACE AND DATE..

NAMES OF THE PEOPLE WHO WERE THERE..............................

....

....

EVENT . . . .

. . . .

. . . .

. . . .

PLACE AND DATE . . . .

NAMES OF THE PEOPLE WHO WERE THERE . . . .

. . . .

. . . .

Accidents will occur in the best regulated families; and in families not regulated by that pervading influence which sanctifies... the influence of a woman... they may be expected in confidence and must be borne with philosophy.

CHARLES DICKENS

EVENT . . . .

. . . .

. . . .

. . . .

PLACE AND DATE . . . .

NAMES OF THE PEOPLE WHO WERE THERE . . . .

. . . .

Do not worry about tomorrow. Tomorrow will look after itself. Each day has troubles enough of its own.

FROM THE GOSPEL OF
MATTHEW 6:34

Schooldays

Well, they're meant to be the happiest days, but there are exceptions; and anyway, happy or not, school can be very hard work at the time! New faces, new subjects, new timetables, success and failure – everything crowds together making us both excited on the one hand and wishing we were at home on the other.

Which schools did members of your family attend? When you ask them, see how many people find their memories make them smile!

Favourite school photo

Multiplication is vexation,
Division is as bad;
The Rule of three doth puzzle me,
And Practice drives me mad.

ELIZABETHAN MANUSCRIPT, DATED 1570

NAME ....

SCHOOL ....

DATES ATTENDED ....

SPECIAL SCHOOLFRIENDS ....

....

NAME ....

SCHOOL ....

DATES ATTENDED ....

SPECIAL SCHOOLFRIENDS ....

....

NAME ....

SCHOOL ....

DATES ATTENDED ....

SPECIAL SCHOOLFRIENDS ....

....

Train your child in the way you know you should have gone yourself.

CHARLES SPURGEON

In everything set them an example by doing what is good.

FROM THE LETTER TO TITUS 2:7

The old order changeth, yielding place to new, And God fulfils himself in many ways

ALFRED, LORD TENNYSON

Our Growing Family

Families change! Before we know it, there are in-laws and cousins and new faces all over the place. These pages may take a little while to fill, but soon you'll have a whole new gallery of family members, and some great new friends!

NAMES . . . .

OCCASION . . . .

. . . .

DATE . . . .

NAMES . . . .

OCCASION . . . .

. . . .

DATE . . . .

Sir, I look upon every day to be lost, in which I do not make a new acquaintance.

SAMUEL JOHNSON

*F*or see the winter is past, the rains are over and gone, The flowers appear on the earth, The season of glad songs has come.

SONG OF SONGS 2:11–12

NAMES . . . .

OCCASION . . . .

. . . .

DATE . . . .

NAMES . . . .

OCCASION . . . .

. . . .

DATE . . . .

Here, there and everywhere

*God gives all men all earth to love,
But, since man's heart is small,
ordains for each one spot shall prove
Beloved over all.*

RUDYARD KIPLING

*Wherever you will go, I will go,
Wherever you live, I will live.
Your people shall be my people,
And your God, my God.*

FROM THE BOOK OF RUTH

The likelihood of an entire family living for several generations in the same area, let alone the same town or village, is now very remote! Casting back over time, we will almost certainly discover that some members of our family have travelled widely. They may have been refugees from another country, desperate to find shelter or they may have left these shores many years ago to start exciting new lives thousands of miles away.

Looking at a map of the world, we may be surprised to find how many parts of the globe have been visited, either temporarily or permanently, by members of our family. What are their stories? Which of them are still there now?

> *I struck the board and cried,*
> *'No more; I will abroad.'*
> *What, shall I ever sigh*
>   *and pine?*
> *My life and lines are free; free*
>   *as the road,*
> *Loose as the wind,*
> *and large as store.*
>
> <u>GEORGE HERBERT</u>

WHO THEY WERE, AND WHY THEY WENT . . . .

. . . .

. . . .

HOW THEY TRAVELLED, HOW LONG IT TOOK . . . .

. . . .

. . . .

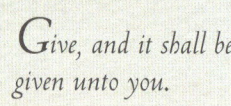

Give, and it shall be given unto you.

LUKE 6:38

Stepping into Tomorrow

One of the greatest things family members can model for each other is 'service'. It begins in simple ways — providing a home, meals, material comforts; also aims, beliefs, encouragement, and guidance. When we leave home, we take with us what we have been given by others. But to be truly free, we must decide what it is right to pass on.

As young people, we can often join service schemes run by schools, churches and charitable groups. To continue in giving, when we are really on our own, is to continue the love of the family in a very special way. Of course, we'll have other plans too, but in this way, wherever we are, the family never really ends. And at the same time, it becomes a new creation.

And I said to the man who stood at the gate of the year: 'Give me a light that I may tread safely into the unknown'. And he replied: 'Go out into the darkness and put your hand into the hand of God, That shall be to you better than light and safer than a known way.'

M. LOUISE HASKINS

Clippings, awards

GROUPS BELONGED TO ....

KINDS OF WORK DONE ....

AIMS FOR THE FUTURE ....

Inasmuch as you did it for the least of these... you did it for me.

JESUS' WORDS FROM THE GOSPEL OF MATTHEW 25:40

I have given you an example so that you may copy what I have done to you.

JESUS' WORDS FROM THE GOSPEL OF JOHN 13:15

Love conquers all things: let us too give in to Love.

VIRGIL

The arrogance of age must submit to be taught by youth.

EDMUND BURKE

May the Lord watch between me and thee, when we are absent one from another.

GENESIS 31:49